Journey to Easter

A Play & Learn Book

Edited by Jill C. Lafferty
Illustrations by Peter Grosshauser

SPARK
HOUSE
FAMILY

Journey to Easter

The resurrection of Jesus is the single most important event in Christian history. It's the reason we go to church on Sundays and celebrate freedom from death and sin. Jesus' followers thought it was a pretty big deal too, which is why they told the stories of Jesus' life and death all over the world. It's why Christians everywhere celebrate Easter every year.

The events that led up to Jesus' resurrection are full of all kinds of drama and intrigue. There's Jesus' triumphal entry into Jerusalem, riding on a donkey as people shout "Hosanna!" and wave palm branches. Jesus has a last supper with his disciples, when he asks them to remember him. Soon after, Jesus is betrayed by one of his disciples and he's arrested and sentenced to death. How could anything good come of this?

This Play and Learn book is filled with the excitement and turmoil of the days leading up to Jesus' death, Jesus' surprise resurrection, and the days following his return. The disciples spread the good news of the gospel for the rest of their lives.

As you and your family explore your Play and Learn book, see if you can find a story where someone:

- Washes someone else's feet
- Eats a meal
- Is surprised or excited about Jesus' resurrection

Each story in this Play and Learn book gives you a verse to remember, some fun activities to try, and ideas for remembering and celebrating Jesus' sacrifice for us. So jump in and discover more about Easter! Christ is risen! Alleluia!

Published by Sparkhouse Family
510 Marquette Avenue
Minneapolis, MN 55402
sparkhouse.org

© 2017 Sparkhouse Family

All rights reserved.

Journey to Easter
Play and Learn Book
First edition published 2017

Printed in United States
22 21 20 19 18 17   1 2 3 4 5 6 7 8
9781506421889

Edited by Jill C. Lafferty
Designed by Tory Herman
Illustrations by Peter Grosshauser
Interior photographs provided by
iStock and Thinkstock

All Bible quotations are from THE HOLY BIBLE, NEW INTERNATIONAL VERSION®, NIV®. Copyright © 1973, 1978, 1984, 2011 by Biblica, Inc.® Used by permission of Zondervan. All rights reserved worldwide. www.zondervan.com. The "NIV" and "New International Version" are trademarks registered in the United States Patent and Trademark Office by Biblica, Inc.™

V63474; 9781506421889; DEC2016

Table of Contents

How to Use Your Spark Story Bible Play and Learn Book

Each section in this Play and Learn book includes a short story from the Bible, followed by all kinds of engaging ways to think about the theme of the story. Look for these activities in every story.

Conversation Starters
Talk about these questions as a family. Make sure everyone gets a chance to share their thoughts.

A Prayer to Share
Cut out these prayers to help you talk to God about what you've learned.

The Story
Start here. You'll get a summary of the Bible story you'll explore on the pages to come.

Explore with Squiggles
This expressive little caterpillar responds to each story with a specific emotion and invites children to do the same.

We are excited about Jesus!

It was time to celebrate Passover in Jerusalem. When Jesus rode a donkey into the city, the people shouted, "Hosanna!" and waved palms to welcome him. But not everyone was happy to see Jesus. Some told Jesus to make the crowd be quiet, but there was nothing Jesus could do. "Hosanna! Jesus is king!" people cheered.

WHAT DO YOU LIKE ABOUT PARADES? HOW DO YOU CELEBRATE JESUS?

JESUS, we are so excited about you! Help us remember to celebrate you each and every day. Amen.

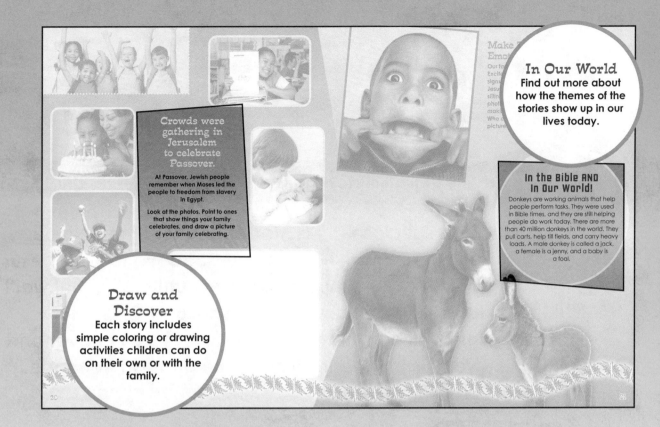

In Our World
Find out more about how the themes of the stories show up in our lives today.

Crowds were gathering in Jerusalem to celebrate Passover.

At Passover, Jewish people remember when Moses led the people to freedom from slavery in Egypt.

Look at the photos. Point to ones that show things your family celebrates, and draw a picture of your family celebrating.

In the Bible AND In Our World!
Donkeys are working animals that help people perform tasks. They were used in Bible times, and they are still helping people do work today. There are more than 40 million donkeys in the world. They pull carts, help till fields, and carry heavy loads. A male donkey is called a jack, a female is a jenny, and a baby is a foal.

Draw and Discover
Each story includes simple coloring or drawing activities children can do on their own or with the family.

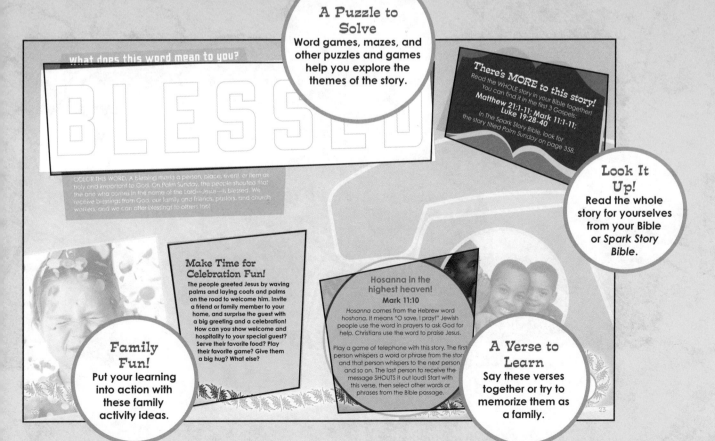

A Puzzle to Solve
Word games, mazes, and other puzzles and games help you explore the themes of the story.

What does this word mean to you?

BLESSED

COLOR THIS WORD. A blessing marks a person, place, event, or item as holy and important to God. On Palm Sunday, the people shouted that the one who comes in the name of the Lord—Jesus—is blessed. We receive blessings from God, our family and friends, pastors, and church workers, and we can offer blessings to others too!

There's MORE to this story!
Read the WHOLE story in your Bible together! You can find it in the first 3 Gospels:
Matthew 21:1-11; Mark 11:1-11;
Luke 19:28-40
In The Spark Story Bible, look for the story titled Palm Sunday on page 358.

Look It Up!
Read the whole story for yourselves from your Bible or *Spark Story Bible*.

Make Time for Celebration Fun!
The people greeted Jesus by waving palms and laying coats and palms on the road to welcome him. Invite a friend or family member to your home, and surprise the guest with a big greeting and a celebration! How can you show welcome and hospitality to your special guest? Serve their favorite food? Play their favorite game? Give them a big hug? What else?

Family Fun!
Put your learning into action with these family activity ideas.

Hosanna in the highest heaven!
Mark 11:10

Hosanna comes from the Hebrew word *hoshana*. It means "O save, I pray!" Jewish people use the word in prayers to ask God for help. Christians use the word to praise Jesus.

Play a game of telephone with this story. The first person whispers a word or phrase from the story, and that person whispers to the next person, and so on. The last person to receive the message SHOUTS it out loud! Start with this verse, then select other words or phrases from the Bible passage.

A Verse to Learn
Say these verses together or try to memorize them as a family.

The Promise of

God promises to love us forever and ever.

Jesus sat close to his friends and told them some sad news. "I will have to say goodbye to you," Jesus said. This news made his friends unhappy. "But wait!" Jesus said. "I'll always love you, and God's Holy Spirit will be with you. God will love you forever and ever." Jesus' friends trusted the promise he made. This promise made them very happy.

Squiggles feels happy. He loves to listen to Jesus.

How does YOUR face look when you feel happy?

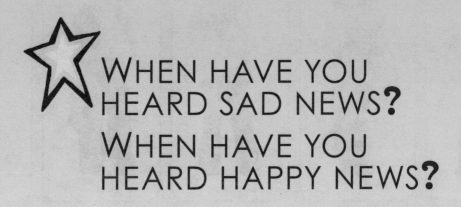

WHEN HAVE YOU
HEARD SAD NEWS?

WHEN HAVE YOU
HEARD HAPPY NEWS?

Cut out this prayer and put it in a
coat pocket. Say the prayer together
anytime you see rain or a rainbow.

THANK YOU for
keeping your
promises, God. Amen.

Jesus shared God's promise with his friends.

The kids in the photos are spelling God's promise to everyone, but they aren't in order! Write the letters in the correct order in the blanks.

God ☐ ☐ ☐ ☐ ☐ you always!

There's MORE to this story!

Read the WHOLE story in your Bible together! You can find it in the last Gospel book:

John 14:15-21

Do You Know? Answers: Wind, flame, dove

Do You Know?

We can't see the Holy Spirit, but the Bible gives us symbols that help us understand what the Holy Spirit is like. Circle the symbols below that help us understand the Holy Spirit.

(See John 1:32 and Act 2:2-3 for clues.)

Make Time for More Fun!

Promise starts with the letter **P**. The next time you are on a car trip, look out the window. See if you can find things that start with the letters in

P-R-O-M-I-S-E.

Before long, the world will not see me anymore, but you will see me. Because I live, you also will live.

John 14:19

Jesus said that even though he would be going away, God's Holy Spirit would always be with us.

Play a goodbye-and-hello game with your family and friends. One person stands in the middle of a circle. The person in the middle looks at someone in the circle and says **hello** or **goodbye**. If it's **hello**, the person in the circle stays put. If it's **goodbye**, the person in the circle faces out. When everyone is facing out, the person in the middle says the verse. Then everyone turns around and waves **hello**. Repeat so that everyone has a chance to be in the middle.

Jesus the Vine

We're connected to Jesus.

Jesus wanted the people who listened to him to know about God's love for everyone. "Think about a vine," Jesus said. "Only branches that are connected to the vine can grow fruit. When you are connected to me in love and you share that love with others, you'll have everything you need," Jesus said.

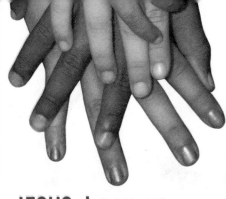

JESUS, keep us connected to you always. Help us to love each other as you love us. Amen.

Cut out this prayer and place it on or near a bed. Before bedtime, have everyone "connect" in a family huddle and say the prayer together.

⭐ **WHAT DO YOU NEED TO LIVE AND GROW?**

WHAT IS YOUR FAVORITE FRUIT?

Squiggles feels interested. He wants to learn more about God's love.

How does **YOUR** face look when you feel interested in something?

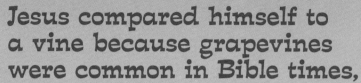

Jesus compared himself to a vine because grapevines were common in Bible times,

and the people listening would understand what he was talking about. Grapes have many uses—they give us a lot of the things we need to be healthy.

Draw a 😊 on the photo that shows the grapes you enjoy the most!

Put a ✓ on other photos of grape products you have tasted.

Grapes

Raisins (dried grapes)

Grape jelly

Grape juice

Dolma (stuffed grape leaves)

There's MORE to this story!

Read the WHOLE story in your Bible together! You can find it in the 4th Gospel:

John 15:1-5, 7-17

Do You Know? Answers: 1. Bread; 2. Light; 3. Shepherd

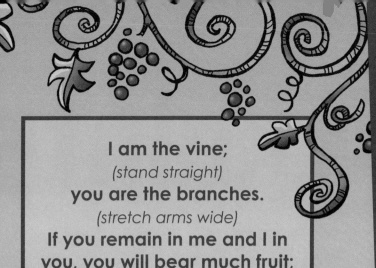

I am the vine;
(stand straight)
you are the branches.
(stretch arms wide)
If you remain in me and I in you, you will bear much fruit;
(cup hands as if holding fruit)
apart from me you can do nothing.
(return to standing)
John 15:5

Practice saying this verse with the actions.

Do You Know?

Jesus often made statements that began with the words "I AM . . ." to help the people listening understand more about Jesus' love. This story includes one of these statements: "I am the vine" (John 15:5).

Use the clues to learn more of Jesus' "I AM . . ." statements.

1. I am the _____ **of life.**
(See John 6:35.)

2. I am the _____ **of the world.**
(See John 8:12.)

3. I am the good _____
(See John 10:11.)

Make Time for More Fun!

Have everyone in your family work together to make a fruit salad. Let each person choose a favorite fruit to add to the salad. Clean the fruit, cut it (if necessary) with adult help, and mix it all together in a large bowl. Now you are connected with one another in a salad! Connect with another neighbor or friend by sharing some of the salad.

Mary Anoints

God's love is overflowing.

To **anoint** means to rub someone else with oil as a way of saying, "You are special to God."

Jesus was eating a meal with friends when Mary anointed Jesus' feet with a bottle of expensive perfume. This made Judas angry—the perfume could have been sold and the money used to help people! But Jesus said that Mary was showing her love the way God wanted. Like Mary's perfume bottle, God's love is overflowing!

Squiggles feels special. God loves him.

How does YOUR face look when you feel special?

14

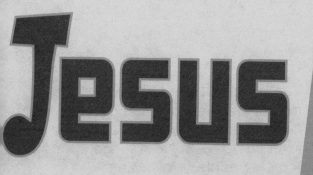

DEAR GOD, thanks for loving us so much. Amen.

Cut out this prayer and tape it to a bottle of lotion. Whenever you use the lotion, say this prayer.

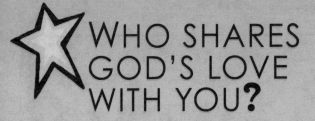

★ WHO SHARES GOD'S LOVE WITH YOU?

WHAT IS YOUR FAVORITE SMELL?

. . . YOU ANOINT MY HEAD WITH OIL . . . YOU ANOINT MY HEAD WITH OIL . . . YOU ANOINT MY HEAD WITH OIL . .

15

In Bible times, people wore sandals, so their feet were dirty almost all the time. Today, we have lots of different ways to cover our feet—but feet still get dirty! Match the people below with the shoes they wear. Whose feet would you be willing to wash? Why?

There's MORE to this story!

Read the WHOLE story in your Bible together! You can find it in the 4th book in the New Testament: **John 12:1-8**

ANOINT MY HEAD WITH OIL . . . YOU ANOINT MY HEAD WITH OIL . . . EAD WITH OIL . . . YOU

Do You Know?

The oil or perfume that Mary used was worth about 300 *denarii*. Denarii were a form of money, like our coins today.

In Bible times, 1 *denarius* was worth about 1 day's wages. It's difficult to compare that to the value of our money today, but some historians assign a value of about $20.00.

If 1 denarius is worth $20.00, then how much was the perfume Mary used worth in today's dollars?

300 denarii X $20.00 =

What could you buy with that much money today?

Then Mary took about a pint of pure nard, an expensive perfume; she poured it on Jesus' feet and wiped his feet with her hair. And the house was filled with the fragrance of the perfume.
John 12:3

Say the verse together while you take turns washing and lotioning each other's feet. Have plenty of towels on hand. How does it feel to have someone else wash your feet? How does it feel to wash someone else's feet?

Make Time for More Fun!

Mary had saved the expensive perfume for a special occasion. Do you have special clothing or jewelry that you only wear on special

occasions? Or dishes and silverware that you only use for special meals? Choose a night for a special meal. Plan the menu. Invite a friend. Get dressed in your very best, and help an adult set the table with your special dishes. During the meal, talk about how God gives us God's best, and how we can give our best to God.

Palm Sunday

We are excited about Jesus!

It was time to celebrate Passover in Jerusalem. When Jesus rode a donkey into the city, the people shouted, "Hosanna!" and waved palms to welcome him. But not everyone was happy to see Jesus. Some told Jesus to make the crowd be quiet, but there was nothing Jesus could do. "Hosanna! Jesus is king!" people cheered.

Hosanna is a word used to praise God.

WHAT DO YOU LIKE ABOUT PARADES?

HOW DO YOU CELEBRATE JESUS?

Squiggles feels excited about Jesus!

How does YOUR face look when you feel excited?

JESUS, we are so excited about you! Help us remember to celebrate you each and every day. Amen.

Cut out this prayer and tape it to your front door. Every time you come home, wave your hands (palms!) in the air and pray it together.

Crowds were gathering in Jerusalem to celebrate Passover.

At Passover, Jewish people remember when Moses led the people to freedom from slavery in Egypt.

Look at the photos. Point to ones that show things your family celebrates, and draw a picture of your family celebrating.

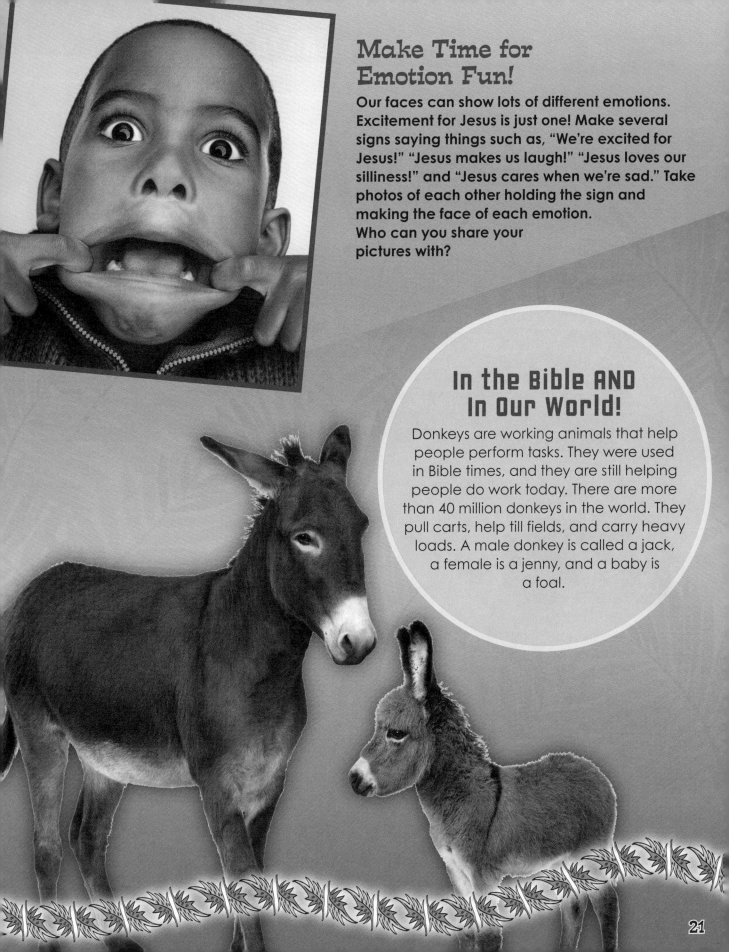

Make Time for Emotion Fun!

Our faces can show lots of different emotions. Excitement for Jesus is just one! Make several signs saying things such as, "We're excited for Jesus!" "Jesus makes us laugh!" "Jesus loves our silliness!" and "Jesus cares when we're sad." Take photos of each other holding the sign and making the face of each emotion.
Who can you share your pictures with?

In the Bible AND In Our World!

Donkeys are working animals that help people perform tasks. They were used in Bible times, and they are still helping people do work today. There are more than 40 million donkeys in the world. They pull carts, help till fields, and carry heavy loads. A male donkey is called a jack, a female is a jenny, and a baby is a foal.

BLESS

COLOR THIS WORD. A blessing marks a person, place, event, or item as holy and important to God. On Palm Sunday, the people shouted that the one who comes in the name of the Lord—Jesus—is blessed. We receive blessings from God, our family and friends, pastors, and church workers, and we can offer blessings to others too!

Make Time for Celebration Fun!

The people greeted Jesus by waving palms and laying coats and palms on the road to welcome him. Invite a friend or family member to your home, and surprise the guest with a big greeting and a celebration! How can you show welcome and hospitality to your special guest? Serve their favorite food? Play their favorite game? Give them a big hug? What else?

ED

There's MORE to this story!
Read the WHOLE story in your Bible together!
You can find it in the first 3 Gospels:
Matthew 21:1-11; Mark 11:1-11; Luke 19:28-40
In The Spark Story Bible, look for the story titled Palm Sunday on page 358.

Hosanna in the highest heaven!
Mark 11:10

Hosanna comes from the Hebrew word *hoshana*. It means "O save, I pray!" Jewish people use the word in prayers to ask God for help. Christians use the word to praise Jesus.

Play a game of telephone with this story. The first person whispers a word or phrase from the story, and that person whispers to the next person, and so on. The last person to receive the message SHOUTS it out loud! Start with this verse, then select other words or phrases from the Bible passage.

The Last Supper

Jesus knew that he would die soon, so he shared his last Passover meal with his closest friends. During this meal, Jesus lovingly washed their feet. He gave his friends a special way to remember him, blessing and sharing bread and giving thanks and sharing wine. Jesus did all this because he loved his friends—and us—soooo much!

★ WHAT MAKES EATING TOGETHER SPECIAL?

WHO WOULD YOU LIKE TO INVITE TO A MEAL?

Cut out this prayer and place it in front of a different person's plate at each meal. That person leads everyone in the prayer before eating.

JESUS, thank you for good food, which makes our bodies strong. Thank you for your love, which makes our hearts grow strong. Amen.

Squiggles feels loved. He knows that Jesus loves him.

How does YOUR face look when you feel loved?

Everyone needs to eat to grow and be healthy.

Eating together helps us feel welcomed and loved.

Look at the photos. Which of these kinds of meals have you enjoyed with family and friends?

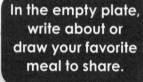

In the empty plate, write about or draw your favorite meal to share.

Cut a large construction paper or cardboard circle into 8 wedges and copy the lines of the Bible verse on the wedges as shown here.

And he took bread,

gave thanks

and broke it.

Luke 22:19

and gave it to them, saying,

do this in remembrance of me."

"This is my body

given for you;

Arrange the wedges correctly and say the verse.

Pretend someone has eaten a wedge—and remove it! Can you still say the verse?

Keep "eating" wedges until you know the verse.

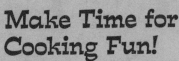

Make Time for Cooking Fun!

Plan and prepare a meal similar to the food Jesus ate. With an adult, enter "Bible times recipes" in an Internet search engine to find recipes. Will you need special ingredients? Make a shopping list! Invite guests to sample your meal. As you eat, share a story about Jesus.

In the Bible AND In Our World!

When Jesus shared his final Passover meal with his friends, he gave them a special way to remember him with bread and wine.

We celebrate this meal in our churches today. It may be called Holy Communion, the Lord's Supper, or the Eucharist. When we gather to celebrate this meal, we remember Jesus and we believe Jesus is with us.

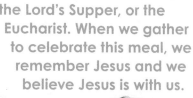

How do you celebrate Holy Communion in your church?

What does this word mean to you?

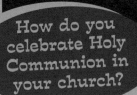

PASSO

COLOR THIS WORD. *Passover* is a major Jewish festival that celebrates God rescuing the people of Israel from slavery in Egypt. The special meal that Jesus shared with his friends, the disciples, was a celebration of Passover. Today, Jewish people may observe Passover with a special meal called a Seder.

Seder is pronounced **SAY-der.**

Make Time for Craft Fun!

Make special placemats to remember Jesus' love. Paste pictures and words that remind you of Jesus on placemat-sized cardstock. You can cut pictures from magazines or draw your own. When you are done, have the creation laminated.

Use your placemats for everyday meals and as a way to share stories about Jesus.

VER

There's MORE to this story!

Read the WHOLE story in your Bible together!
You can find it in all 4 Gospels:

**Matthew 26:17-30; Mark 14:10-32;
Luke 22:14-28; John 13:1-20**

In The Spark Story Bible, look for *The Last Supper* on page 364.

Jesus Is Betrayed

God doesn't give up on us.

Squiggles feels upset. Why won't the disciples pray with Jesus?

How does **YOUR** face look when you feel upset?

Jesus was facing hard times. Instead of helping him, Jesus' friends—his disciples—let him down. Jesus asked his friends to pray with him, but they fell asleep. One disciple named Judas told Jesus' enemies where to find him. Another disciple, Peter, said he didn't know Jesus. But Jesus never gave up on his friends.

HAS A FRIEND EVER DISAPPOINTED YOU?

WHAT DO YOU DO WHEN YOU'RE SORRY?

DEAR GOD, When we are weak, you make us strong. We'll follow you, God, all life long! Amen.

Cut out this prayer and place it on a large, flat rock. Paint over it with glue thinned with water. Let it dry, and use the rock as a paperweight. Pray this prayer together when your family needs strength.

Peter loved Jesus and was sorry that he let him down.

What's happening in these photographs?
What words could help the situations?
Trace the letters with your finger after you talk about the pictures.

I'm sorry!

Do You Know?

When Peter was asked if he knew Jesus, Peter said "No!" three times. But later, Peter became known as a "rock" of Christianity. Which of these things did Peter do? *(See Acts 2:1-21, 36-47; 3:1-16; 11:1-18; and 12:1-19 for clues.)*

1. **Healed people who were sick in Jesus' name.**
   True False

2. **Helped start the Christian church.**
   True False

3. **Built a home out of rocks.**
   True False

4. **Went to jail because of his belief in Jesus.**
   True False

5. **Had a strange dream about animals.**
   True False

Then Peter remembered the word Jesus had spoken: "Before the rooster crows, you will disown me three times." And he went outside and wept bitterly.
Matthew 26:75

Think about Peter's feelings as you color the teardrops in blue crayon. When we do something wrong, we can tell God we're sorry. Circle the name "Jesus" three times to remind you of God's forgiveness. God doesn't give up on us!

Make Time for More Fun!

Make rock candy in honor of Peter, the Rock! Heat 2 cups sugar and 1 cup water in a saucepan. Add food coloring and 2 more cups sugar. Stir until mixture dissolves. Don't boil! Pour into clean jar. Tie a 6-inch piece of string to a craft stick, and lay stick across jar top so string hangs into mixture. Rock candy forms over several days. Retell the story of Jesus and Peter when you enjoy your candy.

There's MORE to this story!

Read the WHOLE story in your Bible together! You can find it in three Gospels in the New Testament: Matthew 26:31-75; Mark 14:26-72; Luke 22:32-71

In The Spark Story Bible, look for *Jesus Is Betrayed* on page 370.

Christ the King

Jesus is King of kings!

The priests wanted to get rid of Jesus, so they had him arrested! The man in charge of prisoners, Pilate, didn't know what Jesus had done wrong. "Are you the king of the Jews?" he asked Jesus. Pilate didn't understand that Jesus' power was about God's love, not about ruling over people. But Pilate didn't want trouble, so he handed Jesus back to the people.

Squiggles feels nervous. Something bad is happening.

How does YOUR face look when you feel nervous?

Cut out this prayer and tape it to your refrigerator. Pray it as often as you get something to eat!

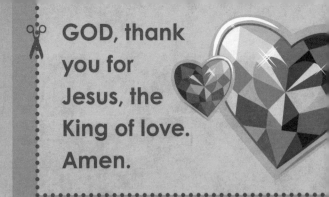

GOD, thank you for Jesus, the King of love. Amen.

WHAT WOULD YOU ASK JESUS?
WHAT'S IT LIKE TO BE MISUNDERSTOOD?

Jesus is the King of kings!

Look at the photos. Some of these things are used by kings who rule over a country. Some of these things are used by Jesus. Circle the things Jesus uses to share God's love with us.

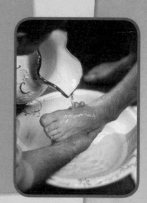

What does this

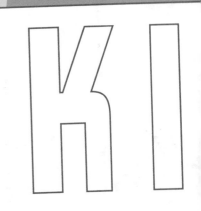

KI

Make Time for More Fun

Make a different kind of crown to remind you that Jesus was a different kind of king. Get construction paper and scissors. Cut a basic crown shape to fit around the head of each person in your family. Use crayons or markers to decorate your crown, but instead of jewels, draw hearts or write words that remind you of God's love.

Jesus said,
"My kingdom is not of this world."
John 18:36

Read the verse out loud together and talk about what God's kingdom is like. Write or draw some of your ideas here:

The kingdom of God is like . . .

There's MORE to this story!
Read the WHOLE story in your Bible together!
You can find it in all 4 Gospels:
Matthew 27:11-31; Mark 15:1-15; Luke 23:1-25; John 18:33-37

word mean to you?

NGDOM

COLOR THIS WORD. God's *kingdom* isn't a single piece of land or country. God's kingdom is about God's love in all the world for all time, and also a time when Jesus will rule with God's love over all people.

The Day Jesus Died

It was a sad day when Jesus died. Angry soldiers put a crown of sharp thorns on Jesus' head. They made him carry a heavy cross. When Jesus fell and hurt his knees, a man from the crowd helped him. The soldiers nailed Jesus' hands and feet to the cross and raised it up toward the sky. The sky grew dark, and with one last breath, Jesus died.

God comforts us.

When someone dies, friends and family often gather to say goodbye at a funeral or memorial service.

There are many parts of a funeral or memorial service that help the people remember and celebrate the life of the person who died. Color the hearts on the pictures that show things that would help comfort you.

SAD TEARS

BIBLE VERSES

MUSIC

FLOWERS

HAPPY MEMORIES

FRIENDS AND FAMILY

PRAYER

Make Time for Flashlight Fun!

It was a sad day when Jesus died. But we know that death is not the end. Jesus came back to life! Grab a flashlight. Go into a room together, close the curtains and doors, and shut off the lights. On the count of 3, turn on the flashlight and shout together, "God gives us hope!"

Surely he was the Son of God!
Matthew 27:54

Using a washable marker, write this verse on each other's forearms. Together, make a cross with your arms and say the verse together.

CRUCIF

COLOR THIS WORD. Jesus died by hanging on a cross. Another way to say this is that Jesus was *crucified*. Two other men were crucified at the same time as Jesus. Each year on Good Friday, we remember that Jesus was crucified. God was with Jesus when he died, and God is with us too.

Today, we don't know the location of Jesus' tomb. The Garden Tomb in Jerusalem is one possible place.

Do You Know?

In Bible times, it was common for people who had died to be buried in a cave, called a tomb. After Jesus' body was put in a tomb, it was sealed with a boulder. Read about Jesus' burial in Matthew 27:57-61. Circle the names of the people who were there when Jesus was put in the tomb.

Matthew

Joseph of Arimathea

Peter

Andrew

Mary

Mary Magdalene

James

IED

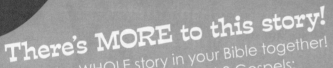

There's MORE to this story!

Read the WHOLE story in your Bible together! You can find it in the first 3 Gospels:

Matthew 27:27-66; Mark 15:21-47; Luke 23:26-56

In The Spark Story Bible, look for The Day Jesus Died on page 376.

Do You Know? Answers: Joseph of Arimathea, Mary Magdalene, Mary

Make Time for Memories!

If you have a friend or family member who has died, go as a family to visit their grave or one of their favorite places. Bring a plant, flowers, or a photo. If you can't make a special visit, remember them by making their favorite food or sharing a story about them. What memories do you want to share about the person you miss?

The Empty Tomb

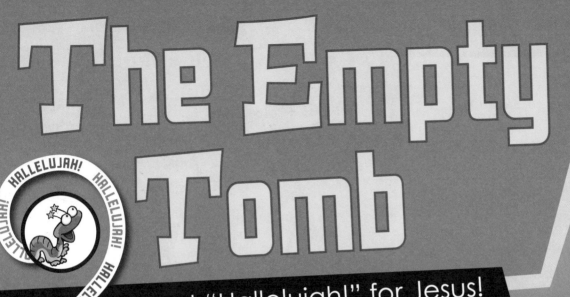

Shout "Hallelujah!" for Jesus!

Mary Magdalene, Mary, Salome, and Joanna approached Jesus' tomb with sadness. It was their job to take care of his body after he died. But when they looked inside, they got a big surprise: Jesus wasn't there! An angel told them that Jesus is alive! They hurried to share the news. Along the way, they ran into Jesus. Hallelujah! Jesus is alive again!

 ## WHAT'S A BIG SURPRISE YOU REMEMBER?

WHEN HAVE YOU FELT JOYFUL?

Hallelujah! We are filled with joy because Jesus is alive! Amen.

Cut out this prayer and tape it to a blown-up balloon. Toss the balloon to one another as you say the prayer.

Squiggles feels joyful. Jesus is alive! How does YOUR face look when you feel joyful?

WHISPER

Hallelujah is based on a Hebrew word that means to praise God.

We sing, shout, and say "Hallelujah!" on Easter to praise God that Jesus is alive again!

There are lots of ways to say "Hallelujah!" Trace the letters, and then whisper, shout, sing, and sign "Hallelujah!"

SHOUT

SING

SIGN

HALLELUJAH! HALLELUJAH! HALLELUJAH! HALLELUJAH! HALLELUJAH! HALLELUJAH! HALLELUJAH! HALLELUJAH! HALLELUJAH!

There's MORE to this story!

Read the WHOLE story in your Bible together! You can find it in the first 3 New Testament books:

Matthew 28:1-10; Mark 16:1-8; Luke 24:1-12

In The Spark Story Bible, look for The Empty Tomb on page 382.

Make Time for Kitchen Fun!

The spices and ointments the women were bringing to the tomb were part of the Jewish burial rituals of the time. Go to your spice cupboard and take turns smelling various spices. Which ones do you like the best? Which ones don't you like? What kinds of spices do you think the women brought with them to the tomb?

HALLELUJAH! HALLELUJAH! HALLELUJAH! HALLELUJAH! HALLELUJAH! HALLELUJAH! HALLELUJAH!

Do not be afraid, for I know that you are looking for Jesus, who was crucified. He is not here; he has risen, just as he said.

Matthew 28:5-6

Use a sheet or blanket to create an "empty tomb" in your home. Reenact this scene. Take turns being the angel who says, "Do not be afraid!"

In the Bible AND In Our World!

After the women found out that Jesus was alive, they **ran** to spread the message by **telling** others. The only way to share the good news quickly was by word of mouth. People in Jesus' time wrote letters too, but letters could take days, weeks, or months to reach their destination. Today, good news is spread quickly around the globe by telephone, email, text messages, and other electronic channels.

HALLELUJAH! HALLELUJAH! HALLELUJAH! HALLELUJAH! HALLELUJAH! HALLELUJAH! HALLELUJAH! HALLELUJAH!

Do You Know?

The phrase "Do not be afraid" is used many times in the Bible. Look up these Bible verses and complete the chart.

	Who said, "Do not be afraid"?	Who did they say it to?
Genesis 15:1		
Exodus 14:13		
Luke 1:13		
Luke 1:30		
Matthew 28:10		

Make Time for Easter Egg Fun!

Collect empty plastic Easter eggs. Write "Hallelujah! Jesus is alive!" on several slips of paper. Fill empty plastic eggs with a candy and a "Hallelujah!" slip. Deliver eggs to neighbors, friends, or family and wish them a Happy Easter!

Do You Know? Answers: Genesis 15:1—God, Abram; Exodus 14:13—Moses, the people; Luke 1:13—Angel, Zechariah; Luke 1:30—the angel Gabriel, Mary; Matthew 28:10—Jesus, the women at the tomb

LLELUJAH! HALLELUJAH! HALLELUJAH! HALLELUJAH! HALLELUJAH! HALLELUJAH! HALLELUJAH! HALLELUJAH!

The Road to Emmaus

We know Jesus lives!

Cleopas and a friend were walking to the town of Emmaus. Three days earlier, Jesus had died, and they were very sad. Suddenly, another man began walking with them. They told the man all about Jesus. Later at dinner, the man blessed bread and offered it to the friends. Suddenly, the friends knew who the man was—Jesus! Jesus was really alive!

JESUS, you really are alive! Help us see you in the world and in our lives. Amen.

HAVE YOU EVER NOT RECOGNIZED A FRIEND?

WHO ALWAYS RECOGNIZES YOU?

Squiggles feels thrilled! He is so happy to see Jesus alive!

How does YOUR face look when you feel thrilled?

Cleopas and his friend didn't know Jesus when he was walking next to them.

It can be difficult to know someone or something when it's very close. Match the photos that go together.

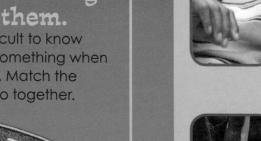

Make Time for More Fun!

Make *cascarones*, or confetti eggs. Hollow out a regular egg, leaving a small opening in one end. Dry the eggshell. Fill with confetti, and glue a piece of tissue paper over the end. Decorate the outside in festive colors. Crack the eggs in celebration and as a reminder that they are empty, like Jesus' tomb.
Jesus is alive!

They were saying, **"The Lord has risen indeed!"**
Luke 24:34 (NRSV)

It is a Christian tradition to greet one another with the Greek phrase **Christos Anesti** (Christ is risen!) and respond with **Alithos Anesti** (He is risen indeed!) when celebrating Jesus' resurrection.

Practice saying these phrases to one another with lots of excitement and joyfulness, and then teach other family members and friends.

Christos = CHRIS-toes
Anesti = ah-NES-tee
Alithos = ah-lee-THOHSS

There's MORE to this story!

Read the WHOLE story in your Bible together! You can find it in the 3rd book in the New Testament:

Luke 24:13-35

In The Spark Story Bible, look for *The Road to Emmaus* on page 388.

In the Bible AND In Our World!

The city of Jerusalem is still an important city in the world today, but the town of Emmaus no longer exists—no one even knows exactly where it was! Based on ancient writings, the distance from Jerusalem to Emmaus was either about 7 miles or about 17 miles. An average person can walk about 3 miles per hour. That means that Cleopas and his friend were walking either a little more than 2 hours, or nearly 6 hours! Either way, that is a lot of walking.

Doubting Thomas

We can believe!

The disciples were afraid, so they hid in a locked room. Suddenly, Jesus appeared in the room with them. Was it really Jesus? They looked at his hands and side and knew Jesus had risen. But one disciple, Thomas, wasn't there. Thomas didn't believe that Jesus was alive until he saw Jesus later with his own eyes. "My Lord and my God!" he exclaimed.

Squiggles feels amazed. Jesus is alive!

How does YOUR face look when you feel amazed?

Cut out this prayer and put it in a hiding spot in your room, such as a shoe box. Get it out and say the prayer together whenever you feel doubtful.

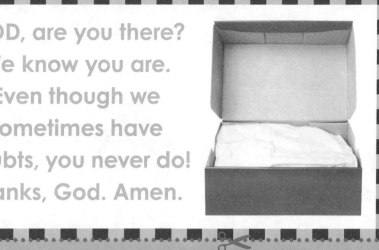

GOD, are you there? We know you are. Even though we sometimes have doubts, you never do! Thanks, God. Amen.

WHO HELPS YOU WHEN YOU HAVE DOUBTS?

WHEN HAVE YOU BEEN AMAZED?

The disciples were afraid before Jesus appeared. They were surprised when Jesus arrived. Thomas was doubtful when he heard the news that Jesus was alive. All of the disciples were happy when they realized Jesus was alive again.

Draw a ☹ on the photo that shows someone who is afraid.

Draw an ! on the photo of surprise.

Draw a ? on the photo that shows doubt.

Draw a ☺ on the photo of a happy person.

Do You Know? Answers: 1. Abraham, Sarah; 2. Moses; 3. Jeremiah

Make Time for More Fun!

Play a game of Two Are True. Take turns saying two statements that are true and one that is false, while family and friends guess which ones they think are true and which one is false. Include true and false statements about this story and other Bible stories you know. How did you know which statement was not true?

56

> Blessed are those who have not seen and yet have believed.
>
> ### John 20:29

On small scraps of paper, write down things that exist but can't be seen, such as wind, music, or laughter. Place the scraps in a hat and take turns drawing one and acting it out without words or sounds. When someone guesses the right answer, shout, "Blessed are those who have not seen and yet have believed!"

There's MORE to this story!
Read the WHOLE story in your Bible together! You can find it in the 4th Gospel:

John 20:19-31

In The Spark Story Bible, look for the New Testament story Doubting Thomas on page 392.

Do You Know?

Thomas isn't the only person in the Bible who felt doubts. Help encourage the Bible characters by filling in their names below.

1. Don't doubt, ☐☐☐☐☐☐ and ☐☐☐☐☐!

   You WILL have a baby.

   (See Genesis 17:15-19.)

2. Don't doubt, ☐☐☐☐☐!

   You WILL rescue God's people

   from Egypt.

   (See Exodus 3:10-12.)

3. Don't doubt,

   ☐☐☐☐☐☐☐☐!

   You CAN be God's prophet.

   (See Jeremiah 1:4-10.)

The Great Commission

Jesus rose from the dead. Soon, he would return to heaven. He told his disciples, "I have important work for you:

Go **everywhere** in the world.
Tell **everyone** about me.
Baptize, and teach them **everything** I have taught you."

Jesus promised that he would always be with his disciples!

WHERE IN THE WORLD WOULD YOU LIKE TO GO?

WHAT CAN YOU TELL PEOPLE ABOUT JESUS?

Cut out this prayer and tape it to a globe or map. Say the prayer together when you plan a trip.

Squiggles feels excited. Jesus has given him an important job!

How does YOUR face look when you feel excited?

Form a family huddle. Say the verse together while doing the actions:

Therefore go
(Turn to face outward from circle.)

and make disciples of all nations,
(Walk away from the circle.)

baptizing them
(Re-form the circle, facing inward.)

in the name of the Father and of the Son and of the Holy Spirit.
(Trace a cross on the forehead of the person to your right.)

Matthew 28:19

Do You Know?

The book of Acts tells stories of three people, whose names begin with the letter "P," who followed the Great Commission to go to different places, tell people about Jesus, and baptize and teach them. Who are they?

HE WENT TO . . .	HE SPOKE TO . . .	WHO?
Wilderness road from Jerusalem to Gaza	An Ethiopian man (See Acts 8:26-28.)	
Caesarea	Cornelius & his household (See Acts 10:22-28.)	
Philippi	Lydia & her household (See Acts 16:11-15.)	

Make Time for More Fun!

Gather family and friends for a relay race. To make a relay baton, write the words of Matthew 28:19-20 on a full sheet of copier or construction paper, roll it around a paper towel tube, and tape. Decide on a racecourse. Before the baton is passed, the giver shouts, "Go everywhere! Tell everyone!" The receiver responds, "Jesus is with us always!"

How do you like to share news? How do you like to hear news?

Look at the photos and color the hearts on the photos that show ways you have heard or told others about Jesus.

There's MORE to this story!

Read the WHOLE story in your Bible together! You can find it in 3 New Testament books:

Matthew 28:16-20; Luke 24:36-53; Acts 1:6-14

In The Spark Story Bible, look for *The Great Commission* on page 396.

The Ascension

The disciples could barely keep up with what was happening! Jesus was arrested and killed, and then he reappeared! Next, before their eyes, he vanished into the sky. But before Jesus left, he told the disciples to share everything they had learned. **The disciples had work to do!**

WHAT AMAZING THINGS HAVE YOU SEEN?
HOW DO YOU SHARE ABOUT JESUS?

Squiggles feels amazed. Jesus gave him a big job!

How does YOUR face look when you feel amazed?

Ascension is the act of rising to a higher level.

GOD, help us tell your story! Amen.

Cut out this prayer and tape it to a ball. Go outside, say the prayer together, and then throw the ball into the air as high as you can.

Jesus wants his message to be shared everywhere in the world.

Draw a line from the picture of the earth to places where you can go to share God's love. How can you share God's love in these places?

There's MORE to this story!

Read the WHOLE story in your Bible together! You can find it in 2 New Testament books:

Luke 24:50-53; Acts 1:6-14

In The Spark Story Bible, look for The Ascension on page 398.

ITNESS

COLOR THIS WORD. To *witness* is to see something and then tell about it. The disciples had seen the events of Jesus' life. Jesus wanted the disciples—and all of us!—to take his message to everyone.

Make Time for More Fun!

The Bible doesn't mention it, but the disciples probably missed Jesus after he went to heaven to be with God. Is there someone you miss right now? Maybe a friend who has moved, a relative who lives far away, or someone who has died? Write that person a letter or draw a picture. Tell about what you've been up to, and tell about the story of Jesus' ascension too.

You will be my witnesses in Jerusalem, and in all Judea and Samaria, and to the ends of the earth.

Acts 1:8

Stand in a circle facing each other. Say the verse together several times, taking a step back each time a new place is mentioned. The good news is spreading!

Matthias the Apostle

God helps us make good choices.

Jesus chose 12 apostles, but now there were only 11. "We must pick someone to replace Judas," Peter said. Matthias and Barsabbas had known Jesus. Jesus' followers asked God to help them make a good choice. God showed them that Matthias was the right person for the job.

Cut out this prayer and keep it in a small bowl on your table. Say the prayer together in the morning while eating your breakfast.

GOD, you know what's right! Help us make good choices today. Amen.

WHEN IS IT HARD TO CHOOSE?
WHO HELPS YOU MAKE CHOICES?

Squiggles feels confident. God helped them make the right choice.

How does YOUR face look when you feel confident?

We can pray when we need to make good choices!

Look at the photos and point to decisions you have made. How do you decide what's right? In the question mark, write a choice you made today.

Gather with your family. Hold your hands in the shape of a heart and say the words of the verse in the hand heart together. Then talk about a decision each person needs to make. How can you help each other make the right choice?

There's MORE to this story!
Read the WHOLE story in your Bible together! You can find it in the book after the 4 Gospel books:
Acts 1:15-17, 21-26

Then they prayed, "Lord, you know everyone's heart. Show us which of these two you have chosen."
Acts 1:24

What does this word mean to you?

POSTLE

COLOR THIS WORD. *Apostle* comes from the Greek word *apóstolos*, which means "one sent on a mission." The apostles were Jesus' 12 primary disciples with whom Jesus chose to share his message.

? ? ? ? ? ? ? ? ? ? ? ? ? ? ? ?

The Holy Spirit

Jesus' disciples were celebrating the festival of Pentecost. *Whoosh!* **A strong wind blew. Fiery flames appeared above each disciple's head. The disciples even started speaking in different languages! This was the Holy Spirit—just like Jesus promised!** With the help of God's Spirit, the disciples started living new lives and telling everyone about Jesus.

Cut out this prayer, punch a hole in it, and hang it near an open window if possible. Talk about the day's weather, and say the prayer together.

HOLY SPIRIT, we can't see you, but like the wind, we know you are here. Help us know your power and peace. Amen.

★ WHO ARE HELPERS IN YOUR LIFE? HOW DO THEY HELP YOU?

Squiggles feels startled. Flames appeared out of nowhere! How does YOUR face look when you feel startled?

The Holy Spirit is with you wherever you go, helping you live God's way.

Look at the photos. Color the flame on the photos that show places where you go. The Holy Spirit is with you in that place!

50

In the Bible AND In Our World!

Pentecost comes from a Greek word meaning "50th day." For Jewish people in Jesus' day, Pentecost was a harvest festival celebrated 50 days after Passover, another Jewish festival. It also commemorated God giving Moses the 10 Commandments. Today, this Jewish festival is known as Shavuot. Christians today remember Pentecost as the day the Holy Spirit came to the disciples! It's celebrated 50 days after Easter.

All of them were filled with the **Holy Spirit** and began to speak in other tongues as the **Spirit** enabled them.
Acts 2:4

The Holy Spirit helped the disciples to speak languages they had never learned so that everyone would hear about Jesus. People who can't hear use American Sign Language (ASL) to communicate. Learn the sign for "Holy Spirit." Then say the verse together, using the sign when you get to "Holy Spirit" and "Spirit."

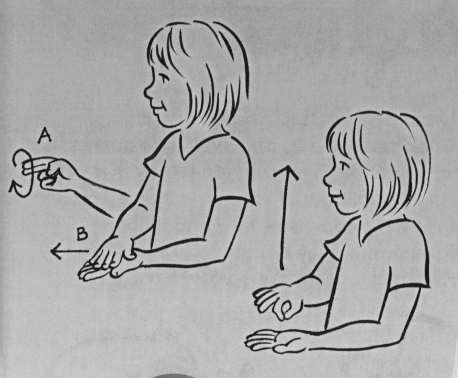

Make Time for More Fun!

Make a Pentecost pinwheel to remind you of the Holy Spirit! With adult help, find a free, printable pinwheel pattern and directions on the Internet. Use red paper to represent the fire that appeared on the disciples' heads. You'll also need scissors, a hole punch, straw, and paper-fastening brads. Make two and share one with a friend and tell the friend about Jesus!

There's MORE to this story!
Read the WHOLE story in your Bible together! You can find it in the 5th book in the New Testament:
Acts 2:1-21, 36-42
In The Spark Story Bible, look for The Holy Spirit on page 400.

Early Believers

We can share God's love.

Early believers in Jesus shared everything: food, clothes, money, and even their homes. There was enough for everyone. They met together to talk about Jesus and thank God. When other people saw how happy the believers were, they became Christians too. **The church family grew and grew.**

Cut out this prayer and tape it to your front door. Say the prayer together before you leave home.

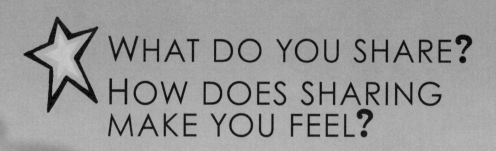

DEAR GOD, help us to share with others so that your family keeps growing and growing. Amen.

☆ WHAT DO YOU SHARE? HOW DOES SHARING MAKE YOU FEEL?

Squiggles feels happy. He likes being with his church family.

How does YOUR face look when you feel happy?

When Christians get together today,

they do some of the same things the early believers did 2,000 years ago: **pray, worship, eat together, talk about Jesus, and help others.** Talk about what the people are doing in the photos. Draw something you do at church.

Do You Know?

The Bible is full of sharing! Solve these riddles to discover people who, with God's love, shared what they had.

1. When there was famine in Egypt, I shared wagons, new clothes, and food with my brothers. Who am I? (Genesis 45)

2. I am a rich man. I shared leftover grain and water with a poor woman working in one of my fields. Who am I? (Ruth 2:1-12)

3. I shared expensive perfume with Jesus when I anointed him. Who am I? (John 12:1-8)

Make Time for More Fun!

Our church family grows when we invite people to our church activities. Who could you invite to worship, Sunday school, or another church gathering? Make some invitations and give them to friends and neighbors. You could offer to help them get to the church and sit with them so they feel welcome.

There's MORE to this story!

Read the WHOLE story in your Bible together! You can find it in the 1st book after the Gospels:

Acts 2:43-47; 4:32-37

In The Spark Story Bible, look for *Early Believers* on page 402.

Do You Know? Answers:
1. Joseph; 2. Boaz; 3. Mary.

And the Lord added to their number daily those who were being saved.

Acts 2:47

When we pray "Your kingdom come, your will be done" in the Lord's Prayer, we are praying that all people will live God's way and love one another. **How can you live God's way and love one another day by day?**

Print a blank calendar page from a computer. Write this verse on top of the page, and talk together about the things you could do. Write or draw some of those things on the calendar.

YOUR KINGDOM COME, YOUR WILL BE DONE...

WILL BE DONE... Y

YOUR WILL BE DONE...

A Note for Grown-Ups

At Sparkhouse Family, we believe faith formation isn't something that only happens when kids are in church or hearing a Bible story in Sunday school. It's an ongoing process that's part of every moment of a child's life. Each interaction with a caring adult shows kids what love looks like. Each playful interaction with a friend taps into their God-given joy and delight. Moments of daydreaming and imaginative play develop their ability to see God in the world.

We also know that many families want to create intentional times of spiritual formation for their kids. That's where the Spark Story Bible Play and Learn books come in. Whether you've already introduced your children to the Bible or are just starting to talk about it, these books make a great resource for helping your family dive into God's Word. They offer a hands-on approach to teaching Bible stories that will resonate with your whole family. Together, you'll explore these stories through games, puzzles, conversation, prayer, and easy-to-manage activities. You can spend ten minutes on a story or a whole afternoon—it's all up to you.

And you won't need a long list of supplies to get started—some crayons, a pair of scissors, and a few items you can find around your house. So make a little time, grab a handful of crayons, and create fun, meaningful family time with God.

Thanks!

Sparkhouse Family

Image Credits

Image Credits (continued)